Leading Groups Online

a down-and-dirty guide to leading
online courses, meetings, trainings, and events
during the coronavirus pandemic

Published by Daniel Hunter. © 2020 Daniel Hunter and Jeanne Rewa.
ISBN: 978-1-67804-133-5
All images are used with permission. Cover, back image, and about authors by
Daphne Philippoussis (instagram @killedmykactus).
Interior pictures are by Jeanne Rewa, except
Finding Steady Ground images by Shreya Shah and
section on honoring people's emotional state by Lunden Abelson.

All content and images are licensed under a Creative Commons Attribution-NonCommercial-NoDerivatives 4.0 International License: https://creativecommons.org/licenses/by-nc-nd/4.0/. In short, that means you may share sections or all of this original
resource as long as you provide Attribution and do not use for Commercial purposes.

Table of Contents

The situation: An introduction 4

The basics: 10 key principles 6
- 1. Be you. 6
- 2. Practice the technology 6
- 3. Minimize people's multitasking 7
- 4. Engage frequently and in varied ways 8
- 5. Manage energy 9
- 6. Honor people's emotional state in this crisis 10
- 7. Track participation 12
- 8. Let people know you "see" them 13
- 9. Oppression is compounded by technology 14
- 10. Release yourself and your group of perfection 16

The tools: online session activities 18

The transition: Moving your plans online 27

The template: Sample slides for a live session 30

The nitty-gritty: Frequently asked questions 38
- What technology should I use for facilitating meetings and webinars online? ... 38
- How can our group make decisions online? 39
- How do we ensure equal access with people who cannot see or people who cannot hear? ... 40
- How can we lead multilingual groups? 40
- What do I do when some people are together and some people are online? ... 42
- The group is going to be very large — over 40 people. How do we handle very large groups? ... 42
- I'm worried about tech problems. How do I react when they occur? 43
- What are common technology problems — and how to fix them? 44

Finding Steady Ground 47

For more resources 52

The contributors 54

The situation: An introduction

Amidst the covid-19 pandemic, teachers, educators, trainers, organizers, consultants, and event planners are being asked to do the same things but online. You may find this a delightful challenge or entirely overwhelming. Maybe you have been in online spaces before — or maybe they're completely new.

As two experienced online facilitators, we rushed writing this booklet to give you some lessons you can use right away.

This is a basic introduction to effectively leading online meetings and events. We bring experience in both formal classrooms and grassroots training, and expect this to be useful to a wide range of people in leading online spaces, whether you call it a training, a meeting or a classroom, and whether you call the people who attend participants, students, or members.

We focus on techniques you can use with any platform (Zoom, jitsi, Google Hangouts, conference calls, GoToMeetings, Blackboard Collaborate, etc). We try to be tech neutral to reach the widest audience. That means you'll have to look elsewhere for support on your particular technology.

Because we're writing amidst a growing global pandemic, we weave in tips and suggestions about how to support people psychologically in this moment. We include a generic agenda that includes appropriate activities, concrete ideas and practices in the always-useful principle of "Honor people's emotional state" (Principle #6), and a resource we've found useful for supporting people in crises ("Finding Steady Ground").

We want to note some things right away:

- **There are plenty of things you can't do online.** We get it. It's not the same. People are more distracted while on a device (multitasking is a real problem!). And the mental load of being in front of a computer is high.
- **People don't do their best learning while under stress.** In normal times, you will always have some participants facing huge personal turmoils and

challenges (housing, safety, going hungry, surrounded by death). But under the coronavirus pandemic, a higher percentage of your participants will be in a heightened state of stress.
- **You have your own learning curve to teach on a new electronic platform.** It's a new bag of tricks to get a sense of the group, adjust to the group, and deliver engaging content. This takes time and practice in a moment when time may be scarce and you may not be in the best place to take risks and learn new things.

Because of that, we have some suggestions:
- **Take a good hard look at your curriculum or goals and expect to do much, much less.** You can't do everything you're used to online. One of the biggest mistakes we see people doing is trying to utilize every moment online by cramming in lots of content. Racing through things online will cause you to lose more people; and detached people online are harder to track.
- **Use this precious space to make connection.** In the face of social distance, these may be some of the rare times people will be connected to their peers and friends. Don't waste that time by assuming it's just about your content. Create space for human connection — acknowledging this may sometimes result in a change of priority for your lessons or meetings.
- **Give yourself a break.** You being uptight or mentally exhausted will do no good for those you are leading online. Laugh at your technology mistakes and be gentle about the inevitable technological snafus. Modeling lightness will be a gift to everyone.

In this moment many of us are making very big changes in the ways we are connecting and working with each other. So much of what we already know from working in person we can (and should) bring into our online spaces, but also there is so much that is different and new!

Even under ideal circumstances, facilitating online can be a challenge. Give yourself — and others — the grace and the space to not be perfect. To learn, make mistakes, try things out. To be caring, compassionate, and patient. So let's dive in!

The basics: 10 key principles

1. Be you.

Leading online is not entirely unlike teaching or facilitating in person. We have yet to find a good educator who can't also teach online. You can do this.

So take a breath and remind yourself of whatever skills you already bring to the table: compassion, a relationship with students, mastery of the content, a sense of humor, gravitas, fluidity, compelling stories. Maybe you happen to be the kind of person who really cares — or handles fear well — or is graceful under stress — or is human. Share that!

You may already know the group. Even if you don't know each person, whatever you know about group dynamics is still true. The group will still have tension, issues of social identity and rank, varied content knowledge, and different people's motivations. Everything you know about how individuals learn still applies. Everything you know about the state of people in crisis is still true.

2. Practice the technology

Whatever platform you use to connect, you and the participants may be learning the technology for the first time, too. If you can, we strongly recommend practicing the technology you'll be using ahead of time.

Set up your video. Make sure your face can be seen. If you're on a phone, find a place to put it down so it's stable. Make sure you don't have strong light coming from behind you. Consider the background, like a plain wall or a semi-tidy view of your house with minimal distractions.

Try out the system. Make sure you can log-in. If you're using headphones (strongly recommended!) or external monitors, test them.

Your group will also need to practice — so plan to teach the technology during the sessions. Obviously that takes attention away from your core content and objectives. But if you don't spend time developing their skills, the lack of skill will keep hampering your sessions. If it's an ongoing group, this is even more true.

Start with the simplest tools. For example in video conferencing, beginning activities might have people share out loud or in the chat box. In a learning management system, start with a discussion forum. Start with the tools that are most straightforward and helpful.

Explain new tools carefully and check for understanding. The first time you use a tool, explain how it will look to them on screen, what they have to do, and how to get help. Before starting the tool, ask for a thumbs up on camera or an "I'm ready" in the chat box. Try to catch early if some people are having trouble — encourage people in every way possible to speak up if directions are not clear.

Offer people a way to get help. Whenever possible, we love to have someone designated as a tech support person. That could be a co-facilitator or a member of the group. When we don't have that luxury, we may give out our cell phone for people to text if they are having tech problems. The software you are using may also offer live help.

Add new tools slowly. Both for yourself and for your participants, use your basic tools in a variety of ways and only slowly add to your toolbox. Adding a new tool often adds energy and interest. Just balance that with the mental energy of learning new technology versus focus on your content or main goals.

Acknowledge it's an experiment. People can also show a lot of compassion when we explain that we're going to try an experiment. "I haven't done this before, but I'm hoping we can try a go-around online..." If it doesn't work smoothly, lightly laugh at it and note how you could do it differently next time.

3. *Minimize people's multitasking*

People on screens are often used to jumping from window-to-window to search the web, play music, and respond to a message. The temptation and likelihood of participants getting distracted or multitasking is significantly higher than when you are in-person.

This challenge should not be underestimated. It impacts every aspect of how we lead online.

This means we have to keep people engaged. Some strategies:

Set the expectation before your session: In emails or posts reminding people about your online session, encourage participants to take steps that will help them have as few distractions as possible. For example, say "When connecting, please join from the quietest place with the strongest internet connection available. If possible, wear headphones or a headset during the session."

Set the tone at the beginning of your session: Naming that distractions are a challenge can help participants pay attention during the session. Even better: invite everyone to remove distractions at the beginning of a session. You can do this in a gentle, playful way. "Prepare yourself to be fully present during the session. Do you need to remove a pet from the room or hide your mobile phone? We won't be using email during this session, so you can close your email inbox, too, if it's open!"

Use the distraction. Are people going to be on their phones? Then encourage them to use the phone to text answers to you. Or if people are going to be surfing the web — then challenge them: "Today we're going to learn about Pythagoras' Theorem. I'll give you 5 minutes to google it and try to figure out what it is and how it is spelled. *Go!*"

4. Engage frequently and in varied ways

The very best way to keep people from going off into other things is to keep them engaged with your session. *Ask questions, switch up activities (not just discussions or lectures), have people journal.* If you engage people in ways that are fun, it will also make them want to stay focused on your session rather than do something else.

As a general rule, we recommend aiming to not have anyone talk for more than 3-5 minutes at a time without pausing for at least a simple engagement of participants.

Make sure you don't always engage everyone the same way. For example, don't always ask yes/no chat questions. People will start to lose interest, especially those who don't prefer that method. For best results, use a variety of engagement types that work for different communication styles and learning styles, and give people options.

Prioritize engagement when you connect live: Check to see if there is information sharing that you could move to outside your live sessions. *For example, could you record a video, share a document, or use email?* Keep in mind the physical and mental challenges of being together live online. Do your best to use this time only for what is most important to do together live, like supporting each other, practicing skills, collaborating, making decisions, social motivation, etc.

Because how to engage people online is such a big topic, in the next section ("The tools: online session activities") we share a variety of tools/activities that work reliably for online sessions.

5. Manage energy

After the first online session we ever led we both experienced a surprise: we were really *tired*. Staring at a screen is a heavy mental load. That's true for you — and it's true for everyone in your online groups. Our tips to manage energy:

Limit session length. If you can help it, we advise that sessions be no more than two hours of consecutive connection at a time. One and a half hours at a time is ideal when you have a lot of participants who are new to the technology. If you have to go through the day, break it up.

Schedule breaks (duh!). *For a one and a half hour session*, you might take *as little* as thirty seconds about half way through to invite people to stretch and look away from their computer or device to rest their eyes, etc. *For a two hour session or more*, giving 5-10 minutes in the middle for people to walk away from their computer and come back is ideal. *For an online event with a lot of sessions*, plan to give people more time to recover between sessions than you might in person. Thirty minutes minimum between sessions is recommended.

Consciously check in with your body during sessions and invite others to join you. Stretch or reposition yourself, close your eyes or look away from your screen. You can even throw on some music and invite everyone to a short dance party!

If you can, give yourself a real break between sessions. *Leading online* is doubly challenging because you have the mental load of staring at a screen *while* multi-tasking to teach, read the group, be on a new platform, etc. We find teaching online more exhausting than in-person teaching. So we plan at least 30 minutes between classes whenever possible — and at least 15 minutes for walking or physically taking a break.

Ask for help. Think of all the tasks you have to do:
- *Facilitate*: listening, asking questions, explaining the next task.
- *Tech tasks*: screen sharing, explaining technology, recording, sharing links in the chat box.

- *Tracking the group*: watching for raised hands, reading the chat box, answering any direct messages.

Consider which of these you can get help with — trading facilitation sessions with a colleague, or recruiting a volunteer or even a member of the group to assist with tech tasks or tracking.

Mix up your participation formats so that both facilitators and participants don't get exhausted by the same communication style. A special trick is to include self-led activities like journaling, drawing on paper, embodiment activities, or reflection activities. Those give you time to take a breath and regroup or adjust your plan.

6. Honor people's emotional state in this crisis

You are going to find people in your sessions tired, angry, and impatient. Stress over life under the threat of covid-19 will cause many to be at odds with loved ones and feel powerless. A good many will be struggling to cope. People are going to be over-stimulated, fearful and reactive.

Whether you're teaching social science, strategizing for passing revolutionary legislation, or organizing community outreach — *every participant is going to bring their emotional state into their sessions.* And in the middle of a global pandemic, that's going to be an ongoing, unrelenting wave.

These reactions are stress responses to fear and threat. Therapist Lunden Abelson explains:

> When our bodies are under chronic stress or facing a traumatic situation, the brain responds brilliantly. Areas of the brain hard wired for protection and survival — the limbic system and the amygdala — kick into gear.

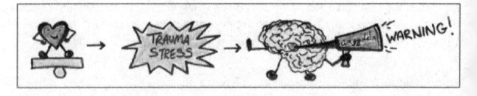

This is an excellent system to have when we need to make a snap decision. Typically when the fight- flight or freeze and collapse defenses come on line they respond to the threat and then when the threat passes balance returns to the nervous system.

However under constant stress our systems run the risk of not returning to a calm state. It's as if an internal stress thermostat is broken — keeping us in a heightened state. This causes us to feel tired, angry, irritable, sleepy, depressed, anxious, hopeless and sick.

When our stress thermostat runs haywire we can lose track of our power and create a grim narrative of the world. *Our sense of personal and collective agency can diminish and we can begin to experience the world as something that happens to us forgetting that we are capable of creating, being intentional, taking breaks and choosing to care for ourselves and our communities.*

I firmly believe that healing happens with increased awareness and the calming of our nervous system — even under awful circumstances. From there people can process how and why we are feeling what we are feeling. With these insights people can mobilize and create change in their lives.

I have witnessed individuals as they steady themselves, identify their fears and claim their power. I have witnessed the growing strength in these individuals as they meet themselves with compassion and ready themselves to translate that steadfast commitment into their communities.

We have already introduced some practices that help with this. Even if you don't feel well-equipped to handle strong emotions, you can:
- Create space for people to acknowledge emotions they have
- Create a culture of checking in
- Model grace and patience
- Use frequent breaks.

We'd emphasize that in the midst of a crisis people often speed up and bring a rate of urgency to every task. *Is getting your microphone fixed really a life or death situation? Take a breath.* Don't work up other people's anxiety.

Here are tools we have used in the past week to help people return to a calmer state:
- Starting with a dance party (throw on music and have everyone dance!)
- Leading people through stretches in their chair
- Starting sessions with music (we used "Miles Davis' Kind of Blue")
- Asking everyone to check-in with a scale of 1-10 of how they're doing
- Opening with a period of meditation
- Not packing an agenda — instead ending 10-minutes early!
- Closing with moment of silence for people's loss
- Closing by having people share one thing they're doing to stay grounded

At the end of this booklet we offer some tips we've used in the past to stay grounded, called "Finding Steady Ground." It's a list of behaviors to help reset our internal thermostat and heighten our sense of agency. We've shared this in online sessions to promote people's staying grounded.

7. *Track participation*

A common challenge in leading online is that we end up in a one-way conversation. We are talking at people, but don't know whether they are learning, whether they agree or disagree, or even if they are still awake! Reading people online is more challenging than in person but it is not impossible.

New online facilitators often try to squeeze every ounce of information from people's videos. You *can* sometimes see if people have their heads turned elsewhere, are typing at the computer, or are smiling/frowning/laughing. But in our experience, what you see from people's video ends up being guesswork — and can be very inaccurate. *Is someone looking away because they're bored, someone walked in, or they're being thoughtful?* Thankfully, there are other strategies:

Include polls or spectrums to gauge responses. Use a live polling tool or ask people to share in the chat or out loud the answer to a simple question or two. You could have multiple choice options visible on screen and read out loud so people can answer simply "A" "B" "C" etc.

Use general check-in questions. "Take a moment to type in the chat: is this clear so far? What's not clear still?"

Review activity between sections. Read posts in your discussion forum periodically. In an extended course, especially, check in more frequently earlier on to see if some people may need more support. As a course continues you may be able to just review a full discussion forum after the deadline has passed or if you have a specific concern.

Ask if your system has analytics. Lots of platforms have different analytical data for you to use to read your group. This could be raw data or different graphs to help you identify trends.

Checking in with people on the phone (especially for tech difficulties). For all of the engagement methods, it's important to pay attention to the people who may get marginalized because of the tech they're using (like, it's harder to use a phone and do interactive stuff, or maybe they're not on video, or...). How you do this may differ according to how large your group is and whether it is an engagement moment where you want to hear from everyone. In general, we suggest inviting participation from people on the phone up front and at the end of an engagement, and leaving a good pause. For example: "Does anyone have any questions before we move on? You can type in the chat or if you are on the phone or prefer to share out loud, you can come off mute. [Get some responses in the chat.] Okay, I haven't heard from several people on the phone so I just want to check to see if you have any more questions on the phone before we continue. I'll pause a few moments so you can come off mute if needed...[pause at least 5 seconds]."

8. Let people know you "see" them

It's one thing to track people. But the more you make it clear that you are reading the group in an ongoing way, the more that people will feel "seen." The more seen people feel, the more they are likely to engage. They are also more likely to send you clear nonverbal signals through their web camera when they get the signal that someone is looking back through their screen.

Here are a few examples of what those signals might look like. The facilitator says:

- "It looks like only about half the group has shared ideas in the chat box. If anyone is having trouble with the chat, let us know, or you can share out loud."
- "I see [name] that you just came off mute. Is there something you'd like to add?"
- "I see a lot of people are saying 'yes' in the chat box, so yes, let's shift to talking about the second topic."
- "I see a lot of heads down on the web cameras, so I'm going to give you a little more time to journal."
- "Everyone has shared except [name] and [name] who are on the phone. Would you like to share, too?"
- "It looks like [name] has stepped away, so we'll come back to them when they're back."
- "Welcome [name], we're just in the middle of sharing one thing we have done that's fun today. [name], [name], and [name] haven't gone yet."

This takes attention but you will be well-rewarded by the effort.

9. *Oppression is compounded by technology*

If you end up tracking participation, you will likely see dynamics of oppression play out. Marginalized groups and those with oppressed identities often tend to participate less frequently. This can become compounded by technology in three ways:

- Oppression hammers people's confidence. As a result, folks' confidence in navigating a novel online space may be challenging. The risk of shaming and exposing ignorance may be much higher.
- People with less resource have less access to high end tech and a dedicated space to work from. Instead of working in front of a large computer with a headset, they might be perched on an outside stoop on their phone as traffic and neighbors pass by.
- People in money-poor areas have largely been abandoned by internet providers. That means people may have inferior internet access. Without high-end high-speed internet, people's connection may be spotty at best.

We're both in poor small-town/rural areas, for example, and have faced the daunting challenge of trying to get stable connections. None of these issues can be fully alleviated without a change in systems bigger than us. So if you're annoyed about it, do join social justice movements for change. Meanwhile, as of print, it appears the big companies are temporarily making access to their hotspots free during this pandemic.

(To be fair, tech also can be an equalizer. Online training can be *more* accessible — like for people who are homebound, people with partial hearing loss, or people in small towns where national organizations rarely go.)

As a facilitator, you have the power to make this situation worse or better.

Don't always pick the quickest response. Instead of picking the first person to say "I have an answer," look for opportunities to support less-heard voices. Make a point of being invitational.

Make sure all people — no matter their tech — can participate fully. Try to always provide alternative options for participation. If someone cannot be on video, make sure there's a way to call-in. If people are calling in, give dedicated space for them to participate during activities and make sure the chat is read aloud. For groups across time zones, this means making sure you don't just offer sessions at times which are good for some people but bad for the same people waking up really early, going to sleep late or working through their regular meal times.

Set people up for success. Another way to cause shame is using right/wrong questions and telling people they're wrong in front of everyone. This can inflame shame. For example, math professors are finding "observation/noticing" methods more effective in their teaching.[1] At the simplest, rather than asking "who doesn't understand this" you can ask "what haven't I explained clearly." This is a pedagogical belief we hold dear — and even more important to do when being online makes it harder to see someone slip into shame.

Think carefully about who can access the technology. As of writing, the Philadelphia School District abruptly halted all online graded activities because they could not guarantee that all their students could participate. This was a technological challenge that could have been averted and resulted in thousands of wasted hours as teachers had already developed new curricula. Some industrious teachers had found loaner laptops for students — but the school district had not ensured access across the board. The lesson is this: if your people cannot access the technology, don't rush — take your time and work to ensure access first.

Offer the space to support people. During this crisis, people are going to have major life issues in front of them. We cannot be sure that our students or

---

[1] Max Ray-Riek's book Powerful Problem Solving: Activities for Sense Making with the Mathematical Practices (Heinemann 2013).

participants are not facing dire circumstances. Especially with on-going groups, create methods to provide checks-ins for people and even mutual assistance, such as:

- Each session have people write how they are doing on a scale of 1-10; use time outside of the sessions to check in with people with low numbers;
- In a safer group, you or your community might have an ongoing list where people can post "Things I have to offer" and "Things I need" — a way to support mutual aid;
- Connect the content to people's currently lived experiences. For a group of organizers: "I'd like each of you to take a moment and write down one big thing going on in your life. Every person you connect with is also going to be having something going on in their life. So without knowing their circumstance, how could you introduce yourself and also honor whatever is true for them? Write down a phrase or two that would be honest."
- Open with moments of silence or guided meditations.

Help make the underlying systems better. It matters to people to see you caring about their situation. Another way to do that is to use time online to link people to groups and campaigns fighting to even the playing field. For example:

- Have people sign petitions asking internet agencies to extend to rural communities;
- Encourage people to participate in upcoming online climate strikes to support a healthy environment;
- Invite the group to support social movements that are working for equal technology access, for expanded paid sick leave, for paid parental leave, etc.

10. Release yourself and your group of perfection

Don't get us wrong — we believe in high standards and excellence in performance. We applaud you if you're the type of person shooting for perfection under all the challenges of this moment. But if you are, then you also need to be ready to aim high and miss.

If you think that your job as a leader of online spaces is to prevent any tech problems from happening, let yourself off the hook right now. There are so many factors that impact our online spaces that are outside of our control (as just one example, bandwidth limitations of rural areas). Prepare yourself for the reality that there will be bumps in the road.

There are things you can do to minimize a variety of problems, but the most important thing you can do is take a deep breath and prepare yourself to stay calm and do your best to support your group through whatever will inevitably come up.

Social distancing and forcibly being confined to home can be challenging. People are struggling, so creating new ways to stay connected is crucial to keeping us strong, mentally and physically healthy, well-balanced, and grounded. Patience, caring, and loving is our most important task, so let's model it with wisdom and intention.

The tools: online session activities

One-way lectures are hard for people to give attention to and make it hard for you to track whether they are with you. So we encourage different methods to keep checking in with people. Thankfully, there is a surprisingly long list of techniques you can use.

Here are a few basic tools/activities:

Journaling

Ask people to individually write on paper.

TIP: In the reminder email and before the session begins, remind people that they will need paper and pen or pencil so they are prepared.

EXAMPLES:

Journal	**Hypothesize**
Think about the story we just heard. How does it apply to you in your context? Take a moment to write down at least 5 lessons learned.	You probably know those Alka-Seltzer tablets that dissolve in water. Which will dissolve faster: one whole tablet or one that is broken up into smaller parts? Take 2 minutes to write down your hypothesis and reason behind it.

Write in the chat...

Almost all video platforms have a method for writing in a chat. This is a simple way to ask a short question and keep engagement lively.

TIPS: These are good for questions that can be answered with a short phrase or sentence. By reading aloud what is being written, it helps affirm participation. You can even notice ("Ted, I haven't seen you writing in the chat. Let us know if you need more time...").
EXAMPLES:

Chat!	Questions?
What's one thing you're doing to keep yourself grounded during this challenging time? *Share in the chat box.*	What's still unclear from the first session? *Share in the chat box. I'll clarify those after the break.*

Individual Drawing

Have people reflect on a prompt by drawing. People can then share their drawings by showing them on a web camera or by photographing them and adding their photos to a shared document or discussion area.

TIP: It helps for people to know ahead of time they may be asked to draw — especially if they might want colored pencils or crayons.

EXAMPLES:

Draw your journey	Graphing practice
If your journey to be an organizer is a river, what's that river like? Draw how your life brought you to this training, with faster and slower parts, sharp bends, etc. *You'll share your drawing in breakout groups.*	Graph this equation without any tech aids: $$y = 2 * x + 3$$ *We'll share the graphs and talk about how you did the graphing.*

Asking open questions

Invite everyone/anyone to share, explaining the various options they have: Type in chat, come off mute, or raise their hand to be called on.

TIPS: Be prepared for some uncomfortable silence after asking the question — it can take a while for people to unmute (or they may try to talk but forget to unmute).

Because quieter people can often become even quieter online, we sometimes encourage participation by asking a question to an individual. "Sheila, what do you think?" It may take people a moment to get off mute.

Therefore, rather than springing someone's name at the end of the prompt, better to say: "Sheila, in a minute I'm going to ask you to answer the next math problem. The problem is..."

This is a great way to support listening and connection by getting people to track who has shared.

EXAMPLES:

Share lessons	Reflect on reading
How can our campaign reach people in a time of social distancing? *Share in the chat box or raise your hand to share out loud.*	What stood out to you about yesterday's reading? *After you share, you choose who shares next.*

Group list-building

Add everyone's answers to a document on screen share, like you might scribe on a whiteboard if you were in person.

TIP: Using a shared document like Google Slides or Google Doc, you can invite people to type their own ideas into the document, or type in chat or share out loud. Otherwise, you can share your own screen and people can see you write up their answers. (Some tech platforms provide a whiteboard tool.)

EXAMPLES:

Lessons learned	**Mutual aid**
What are key lessons you heard from the story I just told? *Share aloud or type in the chat and I'll add to the list.* • • • •	Add your needs & offerings to our shared list. Include your name. Things you need: • Things you can offer: •

Go-around

When you want to hear from everyone in a group, the facilitator calls on each person to come off mute and share out loud until everyone has shared. You need some way to track the order, for example going down the participant list or using a slide on screen share with everyone around a circle.

TIP: Don't do this with very large groups (over 20) or people will tune out. Instead use chat to get many responses at one time.

EXAMPLES:

Go-around	**Test for agreement**

What's your hypothesis about what's going to happen to the liquid?
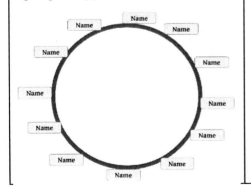
	Each person says *yes, no,* or *maybe* to the current proposal.
	
	Here's an order for our go-around:
	   1. Name
	   2. Name
	   3. Name
	   4. Name

Poll

Ask everyone the same question with simple answers (1, 2, 3 / A, B, C / yes, no / etc.) and invite them to type their answer in chat, or if they can't use chat, share out loud.

TIP: Summarize out loud what you are seeing in chat. When possible, write the results.

EXAMPLES:

You choose	Poll
What topic do you want to learn about next week? A. Writing Poetry B. Writing Non-fiction C. Doing Research *Type in the chat box or share out loud.*	Should we take a break? *Show me thumbs up / thumbs down or shrug.*

Spectrum

This is one of our favorite physical tools, where people line-up along a spectrum. You get to see a range of personal reactions quickly.

Online, you can do this as a poll, only you're asking participants to answer along a scale with numbers at either end, like: 1.......5.

TIPS: Summarize out loud for those on the phone what you are seeing in chat. Describe clearly for accessibility (e.g. people on the phone). Repeat as needed what numbers equal what.

EXAMPLES:

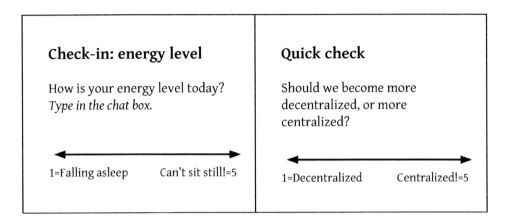

Survey/Quiz

Send questions for people to answer by a deadline.

TIP: Be clear who will be able to see their answers. Will the whole group see an anonymized summary? Will only the teacher see the answers?

EXAMPLES:

Survey	Check-in
Reply by April 14th Which of these factors do you think is the most important for us to consider as we decide on our program's next steps? ☐ Cost ☐ Speed of implementation ☐ Impact	How is the program going for you so far? ――――――――― Rate the workload: ○ 1 - Not enough to do ○ 2 ○ 3 - About right ○ 4 ○ 5 - Way too much

Fishbowl

A tool to have a small group discuss a topic in front of everyone else.

TIPS: Those who are listening/watching can add questions via the chat or respond at the end (such as through a poll).

Make it clear what those on the outside of the bowl should be thinking about or paying attention to, in order to keep them engaged.

Keep the fishbowl rounds short - follow the same guidelines of engaging the full group every few minutes.

EXAMPLES:

Report-back	Going deeper
When your group is in the fishbowl, come off mute and tell us about your book. 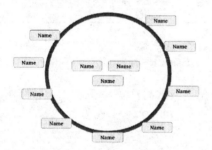 Caption: Image of a circle with names around the circle and several inside the circle.	On the last spectrum we were fairly evenly split into two extremes. *Let's hear out loud from two people on each side of the spectrum. They'll have a dialogue about why they put themselves there.* *The rest of us will listen for underlying areas of agreement.*

Story-telling

Story-telling works very well and needs very little adapting. Stories work when they are personal, specific, and passionate.

TIP: You can add pictures related to your story for visual interest.

Breakouts

You can do many of the same things you would do in an in-person breakout online once you've determined how to do it with your software. Your software might have a built in breakout tool. If not, you can give people separate web conferencing rooms/call lines or have them call each other on their cell phones.

TIPS: It is much harder to check in on your breakout groups online. Therefore:

- Keep your breakout prompts simple
- Be extremely clear about how much time they have and how they will know when to come back
- Make sure everyone is clear about the task — pause before sending people away to see if anyone has a question (make it a long pause)
- Put facilitators in small groups if the topic is complex or you are particularly concerned
- Make sure people are clear about how they can get help during the breakout (text you or message you or...).
- Unless your group is unusually reliable, don't have your breakouts be too long, or you risk losing people to multitasking. 15 minutes is a good maximum unless you have facilitators in the small groups.

EXAMPLES:

Breakouts!	**Pair-Share**
In small groups, come up with the 5 best tips to recruit new members. You'll get 10 minutes. Prepare to report back. If you have any tech problems, call me at 867-5309.	Soon we'll decide on our new program priorities. Discuss your thoughts so far with your partner. Go on mute and then call them on your cell phone. Return in 5 minutes, that's 9:46. Come off mute if you need help and watch for me waving when it's time to come back. If you're ready, type "ready" in the chat box.

Discussion forum

In a self-paced learning tool like a learning management system, invite people to share their answers to a prompt by a deadline.

TIP: Build social connection by including reading and responding to other people as part of the activity expectations. To engage more learning and communication styles, provide the option of posting a video or audio recording instead of text.

EXAMPLES:

Discussion	Practice
Think back to the chapter we read last week. What's one experience in your own life that this reminded you of? *Post by April 1st. Read and ask follow-up questions to at least two of your classmates by April 7th.* > Reply	Now try out the question technique we just studied in a conversation with a friend or family member. You can do this in person, by phone, or by text. Share how did it go? What did you notice? *Post by April 7th. Read and reply to at least two others by April 14th.* > Reply

There are even more ways to adapt lots of other tools to online learning — including role-plays, brainstorming, dot voting, and more. We have more written on the Training for Change website (www.trainingforchange.org) and 350's Training website (trainings.350.org).

The transition: Moving your plans online

You have a lesson or a meeting or a workshop you were planning to lead in person and you just found out that you need to do it online instead. You have little time to make the shift. *What do you do?*

Here's a basic process to adapt an in-person design for online. We offer a template agenda that you are welcome to borrow as a starting point for live online sessions.

Step 1: *Look at your goals, and cut*

Start by looking at what you hoped to accomplish and pare down to the most essential outcomes. This is necessary because of the stresses of the moment we are in and the time your group will need to adapt to the online setting.

Tip: Cut more. You have to make space around the content so you don't replicate rushing and stressing people more. Your content isn't more important than people's mental well-being is it? Cut down your expectations!

Step 2: *Take what you would have done in person and translate to online*

Don't throw away everything you already planned. Use as a starting point your draft or what you are already comfortable leading. Start to sketch out your session flow. The toolkit offers examples you can draw from.

A high percentage of tools can be adapted to an online context. But you'll likely need to streamline the number of activities. Whereas in a face-to-face setting the group could split into pairs, do a task, report-back, and make a large list — online you'll lose time between each activity. Instead, streamline it into something like sharing in the chat and then making a list.

Step 3: Check for best online practices

Assess your draft with our top tips (Are you managing energy? Is it honoring people's emotional state? Are you using varied tools?).

Make adjustments as needed, using the sections above for more details.

- ❏ Are you opening, closing, and pacing in a way that is honoring people's emotional state?
- ❏ Are you taking steps early on to minimize multitasking?
- ❏ Are you engaging the group some way every 3-5 minutes?
- ❏ Are your engagement methods varied?
- ❏ Do you have enough breaks built in – for you and for the participants?
- ❏ Have you built in ways to track the group?
- ❏ Are you prioritizing using live time for connection?

Advanced Tip: Prepare visuals

We didn't want to freak you with too many tool options. But if you have the time, you can create visuals to go along with each tool. If you're presenting a session live, you can screen share and people both see the task and hear the task. We include some examples in the toolkit, but actually we recommend doing this for virtually every tool. That's because some people are visual learners — and if they're just looking at your face, it's easy to lose track of the task. This also helps people with spotty internet who may miss something said out loud.

Using visuals engages participants with multiple learning channels and increases the accessibility of your sessions. Visuals can also help simulate online the tools or physical spaces we might use in-person, such as a drawing of a table where people put their names at a seat or circles representing parts of the room to meet for breakout groups.

Step 4: Prep your session(s)

Set up your session tech. This may be scheduling a video chat (like on jitsi or Zoom) or it may be setting up the whole thing in a learning management system. If you haven't picked your tech, we offer a few suggestions in the *For More Resources* section.

Prep for any additional set-up based on the activities you have planned, and share the information with your group about how to connect and what to expect. If you're concerned about any parts of your plan, do a practice run through, ask for help, or prepare a plan B.

Line up support: If you can, find someone to support you by sharing the mental load involved in leading online. If there isn't anyone who can work with you during your session, find out what other help you have available (software help lines, on-demand resources, etc.) and have that information handy in case you need it.

Set up your space: The ideal setup includes a quiet place (reduces background noise and distraction), headphones or a headset (to reduce background noise and audio "feedback"), good lighting (so you can see each other). Clear the area of anything that might distract you or tempt you to multitask. Check your ergonomics, especially if you will be there for a long time. Gather things that will support you physically and mentally to be relaxed and present. For example, snacks, hot beverages, something that makes you smile or reminds you of why you do what you do.

Tip: If you're going to do live sessions a lot, having two computer screens can help you keep an eye on all the different tools at once. Keeping your meeting/training outline and notes on paper in front of you can also help you manage your screen space.

The template: Sample slides for a live session

Here's the basic outline of an online session we might lead. We often create slides which we display on screen share to help focus participants. In this section are sample opening slides to guide people in the time of covid-19, examples of how we might lead interactive tools, and example closing slides. We also start with some tech slides to make sure people are set-up for the activities.

You can download a copy of this Google Slides template (bit.ly/lgo-template). Feel free to edit and use these slides for your online sessions.

Introduction to Tech Slides

These are tech slides we might show at the beginning of a session. Which things are helpful to show people depends on your software and how you plan to engage participants.

Here are a few examples we use in Zoom.

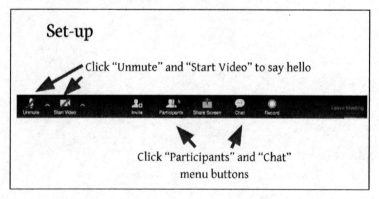

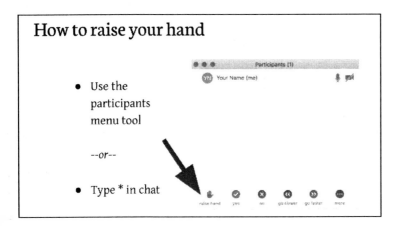

Generic Opening Slides

These are opening slides we have been using during the global pandemic. We don't use all of them at once. Select those most appropriate to your group.

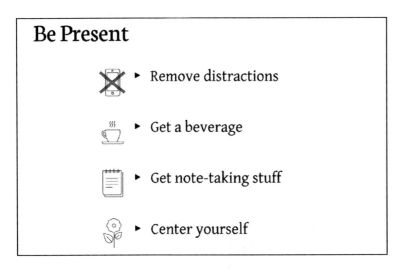

Grab an object that supports you

Find a close-by object that expresses a strength you bring to this gathering right now...

Requests for this call

We're going to gather together online. Therefore, you may have wishes to your colleagues about the kind of space we create. *Write any requests you have on the list below. Affirm any requests by dragging and dropping a star onto it.*

-
-
-
-
-
-

Dance!

Everyone mute and start the video (then press pause so it's buffering).

I'll count down to 0.
Then everyone press play at once.

Then we dance!

Main Content: Tools

These are slides we use to kick-start different interactive tools.

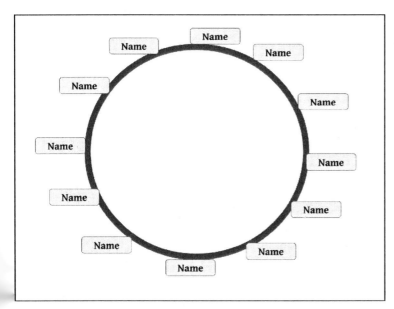

[PROMPT] *Double-click a post-it to edit.*

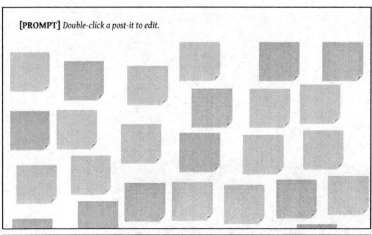

[PROMPT]

-
-
-
-
-
-

-
-
-
-
-

Drag and drop to put your name on the spectrum:

[PROMPT]

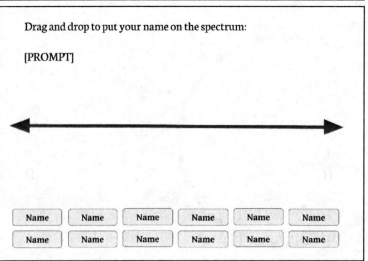

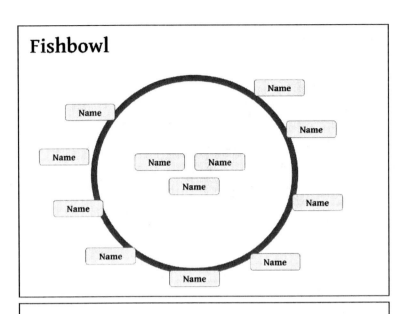

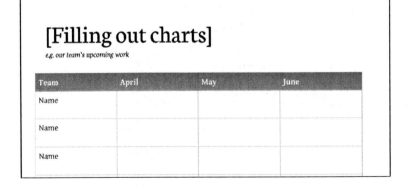

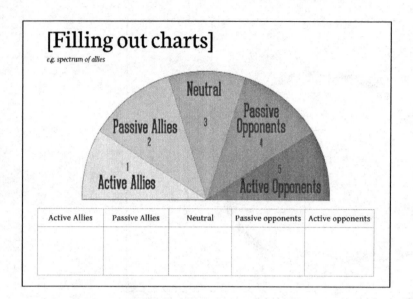

Generic Closing Slides

A few recommendations of possible ways to check-out, especially in light of people's current emotional states.

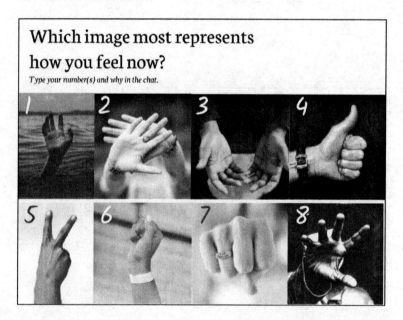

Check-out

In the chat, write down one thing you're going to do to help ground yourself right now.

The nitty-gritty: Frequently asked questions

What technology should I use for facilitating meetings and webinars online?

If you're in the situation where you need to decide right now what to use, here are a few tips to get you started:

Always start from your goals: *What are you trying to achieve? For example, is social connection very important to you? Do you need to be able to grade people's work?* List tools you think will be most important. Starting this way helps you avoid the situation where you chose software just because it was popular or looked good only to find out it couldn't do what you need.

Understand your group's needs: Before you choose software, get clear on the needs of your group. *Do you need software that works well with screen readers? Do you need a conferencing platform that will allow people with no internet to call in by phone? Does your group have specific security needs?*

Search based on your requirement lists: Take the list of requirements you've created from the previous two steps, plus your budget, and search for software that might meet these needs. At this point you might check the software that other people you know use, to see if it has the features you are looking for. If you are considering software with a low price tag, check to make sure that it has the kind of reliability and tech support that is needed to make it a solid choice.

Try it out. Lastly, try out any software before you use it. Keep in mind who your group is and make sure that the software will be easy to use and accessible for them before you buy.

Three online meeting systems we regularly use for live sessions:

- **Zoom (zoom.us)**: reliable for big online meetings; its free (basic) version allows 40 minutes and up to 100 participants; requires an easy software

download to use; can do higher encryption; free for school teachers; includes breakout rooms;
- **Jitsi (jitsi.org):** a completely free open-source platform built for security; very easy and quick to set up calls — no software download for computers (but phones need to download an app); gets more unreliable for larger groups (10+);
- **Skype (skype.com):** reliable for small ongoing meetings; software is simple to set up; it is free (with paid features); less digitally secure; requires an account to connect.

How can our group make decisions online?

Making decisions with a group is challenging enough in person. Online a common dynamic we see is that people fall into a pattern of treating silence as agreement. Most of us wouldn't have to think long to remember a time when our silence in a decision-making process was not because we agreed! When our work is moving to remote spaces, it's crucial that the quality of our decision-making doesn't fall off just because we are doing it online.

Here are some key lessons we've learned for making quality decisions online:

Hold on to the decision-making processes and values you already have. If your group is used to making decisions based on consensus, don't just change to majority-based voting because you're moving online. Make your existing values and processes work.

Rely less on non-verbal cues. We've already noted the challenges of reading people nonverbally online. It's especially important to use a range of ways to read your group when making decisions online. Instead use polls, the chat, or verbal affirmations.

Use an opener to get people talking before you jump to decision-making. Often there are things under the surface that a group needs to work through before they are ready to make a solid decision that they can get behind. Online it can be much harder for the group to naturally break the ice and start those conversations. You can help by setting up an activity that helps the group get a sense of where each other are and gets people talking more easily. Some examples include using a spectrum to see where the group is leaning/feeling, doing breakouts in pairs, starting with some journaling, doing a sentence completion go-around.

Hear from everyone. When it comes time to make your decision, use a participation format that ensures each person contributes, and no one's silence is assumed to mean they agree. Some options are: do a go-around, have one person share and they pass to the next person and so on until everyone has shared, ask everyone to share in chat or out loud and track that each person has responded, or use a polling tool.

How do we ensure equal access, especially with people who cannot see or people who cannot hear?

Leading groups online offers some new challenges but also many benefits for access and engagement of people with disabilities. The choices you make can help maximize those possible benefits.

Become familiar with the accessibility features of the software you are using and share that information with your group.

If at all possible, try to find out the needs of members of the group ahead of time. Someone who is deaf may have an interpreter, may be able to effectively read lips, or neither. Each situation requires different levels of adaptation.

Give people choice about the ways they share information. For example, in a live session, give people the option to share out loud or in the chat box. Then make sure to read everything from the chat aloud. When recording videos use closed captioning or offer a transcript.

Support people's choices about how and where they connect. For example, some people may be more able to be present and engaged if they can connect from bed or with their camera off.

When creating visuals, check that they are accessible and give people direct access to them (not just showing them on screen share). Use captions on images — and if there aren't captions, make sure the images are verbally described.

How can we lead multilingual groups?

We have led non-simultaneous translated sessions and they are... painful. They can be done but they take over twice as long. Further, it's very hard to keep up a flow of conversation.

If the group doesn't have to interact frequently, you can have people work in separate breakout rooms or channels and then come together occasionally. But then people don't get to benefit from each other's wisdom.

Thankfully, most technology platforms offer more options.

Zoom, for example, offers a way for meetings to have simultaneous translation (bit.ly/lgo-zoom), where individuals can select their preferred language. This requires one or two dedicated interpreters. Similar options exist on other platforms.

There are apps that claim to provide *automated* simultaneous translations. But we have yet to find one that works well. They all fail mightily on consistency and are terrible with accents. We don't recommend pursuing this option.

Whatever you use, we recommend:

- Sending materials to participants in advance, sharing the agenda and any materials in all your official languages at the same time.
- Including in your pre-meeting information what the dominant language of the training will be (if applicable), and any additional language support that will be included, such as interpretation.
- Including software connection instructions in all needed languages. If the help guide for the software is available in multiple languages, make that clear and share a link. If you will have international callers dialing in by phone, provide international call-in numbers.
- Writing instructions for activities increases the comprehension of your instructions across languages, so prepare slides to share during your meeting or training that include simple instructions for all activities.
- Preparing any visuals you are using for the meeting to include all present languages, if possible.
- If you will be working with an interpreter or interpreters, sharing your materials with them in advance and answer any questions about your terminology or your software. Do a run-through if possible to get used to both your content and the software.
- Making norms very explicit at the beginning — such as how interpretation will happen, one person speaking at a time, creating signals to ask for tech help/interpretation assistance.

What do I do when some people are together and some people are online?

When some people are joining from a room together and others are at their own computers, facilitators usually need to be more direct and specific with instructions to make things work. For example, you might invite specific people to share, ask people to help you out in a specific way, tell people how you want them to form groups for breakouts, etc. If this is a group you are used to facilitating in a less directive way, you may want to let the group know that you will be shifting your facilitation a bit to help make sure everyone is able to participate fully.

Set up groups so people can be seen: When everyone is joining, encourage people joining as a group to move their camera and chairs to show as many people as possible on camera, as large and clearly as possible, on camera. Ask them to place the web camera near where they see the people on screen, so that it will be as close as possible to eye contact.

Write the names of every person: If the names of the people connecting individually are too small to see on screen for those connecting as a group, have someone write those names up on a whiteboard or chart paper in their room.

OR, Use the "Circle Up" tool to put all participants around one big virtual circle. Ask participants to draw a circle on their own paper while you show it on screen share with a slide. When you add a group of people in the same room to the circle, put them all near each other on the circle, sitting in the same order they are sitting in their room on camera. Throughout the session, both you and participants can use this as a reminder of who is "in the room."

Offer different ways people can be heard. At the beginning of your session, make sure everyone knows how they can get their voice into the room.

Be aware of the mental load imbalance: For people next to people, there's a certain positive energy. For people online, they'll need more breaks, find it harder to concentrate (and easier to be distracted), and appreciate more explicit invitations.

The group is going to be very large — over 40 people. How do we handle very large groups?

For very large online sessions (40+ people) it's important not to lose your focus on engaging the group frequently and in varied ways. The keys to managing multitasking and distractions may be even more important in large online groups than in small ones. In general, with large groups online you'll be using a slightly more narrow list of tools in order to avoid those that require more technical support, and you won't count on tracking that everyone is participating.

You can use many of the tools listed above, but you might adjust in these ways:

- Don't do any activities where you have every single person share out loud (like a go around)
- Don't count on tracking that every single person has participated in an activity
- Rely especially on different methods of engaging that require no special technology (journal, story-telling, guided visualization) or those that use the chat box plus out loud (poll, spectrum, group list-building, brainstorm, fishbowl)
- Breakout groups may need to have more people in them, so there are not a huge number to manage (especially if you have facilitators in the breakout rooms, too)
- Utilize asynchronous tools. So for example with list-building, start your list before a session and/or continue it after a session using self-paced tools like surveys, collaborative documents, etc. The same applies for voting. The key here is that it takes the pressure off of resolving all technical challenges during a session or having enough time for everyone to input during a live session.
- Have extra technical support, like chat box moderators.

I'm worried about tech problems. How do I react when they occur?

Technological bumps are unavoidable. If you can, get to know your specific software for additional challenges and strategies to solve them.

General principles that can be applied no matter what the software or the problem:

Hold the space: As a facilitator, your tone and direction impact the group, so when problems arise, keeping a calm tone while you work things through is very helpful. Humility and vulnerability can help, too!

Utilize your co-facilitator: Help keep the group on track by having one of your facilitators, or your tech support person, work on the issue while the other holds the space. Here are a few examples of what this might look like:

- "I see [participant] is having trouble connecting. [Co-facilitator], can you connect with them, while we keep discussing?"

- "I see [participant] is having some trouble with their microphone. It looks like [Co-facilitator] is going to work it out with them in [private chat / a breakout room], while the rest of us keep talking."
- "I'm having some trouble with my connection. [Co-facilitator], can you take over for me for a couple minutes while I move closer to my wifi-router?"

Take a pause: Just like with in-person meetings, facilitators may need to take a moment to figure out what to do in a situation. It's okay to say "Let's take a 5 minute break then come back" or give participants a breakout activity or a journal activity or something like that which moves the agenda forward but also gives the facilitator(s) an opportunity to regroup or deal with the issue.

What are common technology problems — and how to fix them?

Challenge: Background Noise

Prevention:

- Set a norm that everyone should be muted when they are not talking (including facilitators), unless your group is very small
- Encourage everyone to connect from a quiet space and wear headphones

In the moment:

- Say you are hearing background noise and ask everyone to mute themselves. This often doesn't work, though, so you may have to:
- Use your host control in your software or conference call line to mute specific people or mute everyone (this is especially helpful if you don't want to interrupt someone who is talking in order to ask others to mute)

Challenge: Audio Feedback
(that awful screeching caused by a microphone picking up what is coming out of the speakers)

Prevention:

- Ask everyone to use headphones or headset (including facilitators!)
- Set a norm that everyone should be muted when they are not talking (including facilitators), unless your group is very small

In the moment:

- First stop the screeching by using your host power to mute everyone (including yourself). Then selectively un-mute. If it starts again you've identified the person who is the problem. Make sure they are wearing headphones or a headset. If that is not possible, make sure that everyone else is muted whenever this participant talks (including the facilitator).

Challenge: Trouble turning on microphone or video

Prevention:

- Ask everyone to connect 10 minutes before the call. Use this time to ask people to come on camera and off-mute so you can troubleshoot now.
- Include help slides about turning on microphone and video and the audio/video settings in your meeting slides and/or send to participants through email.

In the moment:

- Confirm they actually have a microphone or camera on the device they are using. Then, make sure they know how to turn on microphone and video and that they are trying that. If that doesn't work, they should go into their audio/video settings to make sure the right microphone or web camera is selected. If yes, but it's still not working, try restarting the software or restarting their computer.

Challenge: Trouble connecting

Prevention:

- Make sure instructions were sent well in advance as well as just before the call.
- Include instructions on where to download the software for those who haven't used it before.
- Encourage people to connect from a location with the highest speed internet they have access to.
- Include phone connection information whenever possible (and selection of software that allows a phone connection is recommended for maximum inclusion)

In the moment:

- Ideally have one co-facilitator support this person while the other holds the meeting. This could mean talking with them through email or text, or getting on the phone with them.

- Resend connection information.
- Make sure they are connecting from somewhere with internet access or phone signal (as applicable) and that they have the software installed.
- Restart their device and try again.
- If the trouble continues, connect them to the help guide/staff for the software you are using.

Challenge: Poor connection / Getting disconnected

Prevention:

- Encourage everyone to connect from the strongest internet connection they have access to. *Ideally* wired/ethernet, rather than wireless.
- Have phone connection information available as a backup or for those without internet access.
- Encourage everyone to limit bandwidth usage by restarting their computer before the call and closing any applications they will not be using during the training.

In the moment:

- Check internet access/strength. Move to a location with stronger connection (for example move closer to a wifi router) if needed.
- Try restarting your device or connecting with a different device.
- Try not using web camera and/or having everyone turn off their web cameras to reduce the bandwidth used in the call.
- Connect by phone instead (note that sometimes phone/cell signal is weaker than internet bandwidth, so this is not always the best solution).
- Consider who is getting disconnected and how often; be prepared to move to a plan B (like everyone move to conference call line) or to reschedule your call (for example a key participant in a decision is on the phone while traveling through a mountainous area and does not have a reliable connection).

Finding Steady Ground

To be in shape for the long haul, we have to keep our minds and spirits ready and our hearts open.

When we're in bad shape, our power is diminished — we're less creative, more reactive, and less able to plan strategically. If we intend to stay active and effective in the world, we have a responsibility to tend to our spirits.

Here are 7 behaviors we can use to strengthen ourselves, so we can keep taking more and more powerful and strategic actions.

1. I will make a conscious decision about when and where I'll get news — and what I'll do afterwards.

What you choose to pay attention to during the day has an impact on you. Which news sources help you understand the world more fully, and which ones only leave you fearful and despairing? After getting your news, what works for you: moving your body, talking with friends, hopping onto social media? Make it conscious — and if it doesn't work, don't keep doing it.

Many "news" sources are designed to trigger fears, sell products, create an addiction to that source, or reinforce pre-existing beliefs. Our goal is to understand what is happening in our world fully enough to be able to engage with it. Much of the information we need comes not from the news, but from the world around us, i.e., observable natural and human capacities, so it is critical to pay attention to those as well.

2. I will make human-to-human connection with another person and make sure we stay in motion.

The goal is accountability, so that we don't freeze in the face of overload or despair. Check in to share and reflect on how you are staying in motion (like writing letters, volunteering, creating resistance art, working on virtual campaigns). As we face increasing social isolation with COVID-19, we may have to work harder for this contact, and it is more important than ever. Formal meetings or facilitated spaces can be moved online. If we can't physically be in touch with people, then we need to get creative—with virtual dinner tables, phone calls, video chats, distance walking or even writing! Whatever we do, we must resist social isolation.

A natural response to conflict is to fight, flee or freeze. In the right context these instincts can lead to survival. Recognizing when you are frozen is important because the longer you stay stuck the harder it is to move, take care of yourself, and be an agent of change. Of course, the goal isn't just a fight or flight survival response, but linking that to our higher brain functions. The support of others helps us do that.

3. I will pray, meditate, or reflect on those I know who are being impacted by oppressive policies, and extend that love to all who may be suffering.

Learn to cultivate love. One starting point may be holding compassionate space for your own pain or the pain of those close to you who are being impacted by the policies and politics of the time. In that reflective space you can give yourself space to be, feel loss, grief, anger, frustration, helplessness, and conviction. Then hold your love and extend it beyond, to others you may not know who are also suffering. And lastly, take time to notice that this is not all of your reality: you also may have joys with your folk around you, be surrounded by beautiful music or nature, and take delight in creation. Joy in the face of hard times is not a luxury, it is a necessity.

We have to learn to hold the emotions of these times, and continually grow our hearts to be in touch with the suffering of others, both within and beyond our own circle. Without extending our love to others, we are in no spiritual position to defend and struggle with them.

4. I will read, listen to, or share a story about how others have survived and resisted injustice.

Millions have faced hard times and injustices and we all can learn from them. Stories may be from ancestors, contemporaries in this country, or lessons from those around the globe who have faced more severe and repressive governments. The goal is to become a student of history so that you can take inspiration and deepen your understanding of how to struggle and thrive.

To find stories, seek out elders in your community, activists who have been in the trenches, and people who have lived through injustice. A few online resources for stories (all these except the first are available in multiple languages):

Case studies
- Global Nonviolent Action Database (nvdatabase.swarthmore.edu), example of campaigns from around the globe
- Beautiful Rising (beautifulrising.org), stories and tactics from around the globe

Online Films
- A Force More Powerful (www.aforcemorepowerful.org), 6-segments of global social movements
- Bringing Down a Dictator (www.nonviolent-conflict.org/icncfilms), video of how people power in Serbia overthrew their dictator

Online Courses
- 350's Online Skill-ups (trainings.350.org/online-skill-ups), online courses about organizing, social movements, and more

5. I will be aware of myself as one who creates.

The goal of injustice is to breed passivity — to make us believe that things happen to us, events happen to us, policies happen to us. To counteract this, we need to stay in touch with our sense of personal power. One goal is to see ourselves as people who create, whether it's cooking a meal, organizing a dazzling dramatic action, knitting a hat, making a sign, or playing the piano. We are more than consumers, and our humanity must be affirmed.

6. I will take a conscious break from social media.

Instead, fill the time with intentional and direct human interaction. You could take a full day a week away from social media as a healthy minimum, but you decide what is right for you.

The research is clear: staying on social media leads to more anxiety, more disconnection, and more mental distress. The exposure to graphic images and reactionary language too often keeps us in our reptilian (fight or flight) brain. That's not to deny the power of social media, but for our own well-being, we must find healthy boundaries.

7. I will commit to sharing with others what's helping me.

This is not meant to be a complete list, but rather a baseline for maintaining emotional well-being in hard times. These are keystone behaviors that can help generate new patterns and consciousness. Share this list with others and add your own to it, creating a commitment to health and building accountability as we strive for a better world.

We provide these commitments on our website: FindingSteadyGround.com in downloadable form so you can post them on your wall.

Find these helpful? Get reminders, more encouragement, and updated resources from FindingSteadyGround.com.

(Credit for Finding Steady Ground: Daniel Hunter pulled together a team of activists, radical healers, and elders to generate this list — initially sparked by a conversation with Lunden Abelson. We were motivated to do this by the number of people we saw in bad psychological shape. It's been a team effort: Shreya Shah of SaltWaterTraining.org designed the beautiful artwork, Kaytee Ray-Riek assisted with social media outreach, Matthew Anderson designed the website, and Pamela Haines wrote text and copy-edited.)

For more resources

More interactive online tools

Training for Change: an excellent source of tools, handouts, and articles on online facilitation: bit.ly/lgo-tools

Trainings.350.org: bit.ly/lgo-350

Template of Online Session, all slides from the template: bit.ly/lgo-template

Workshops to gets more hands-on support

Online Training Series: Training for Change workshops on how to lead sessions online, bit.ly/lgo-trainings

If you want to strengthen your skills on becoming an activist, 350.org has some great online skill-ups you can take: bit.ly/lgo-online

Leading "hybrid" meetings
(some people in-person and others online)

Facilitating Hybrid Meetings Online: bit.ly/lgo-hybrid-online

Accessibility

Web Accessibility Initiative's tips for building accessible web resources: bit.ly/lgo-accessibility

Articles on facilitating online

Online tools, templates, handouts, and videos in English & Spanish (e.g. Quick Guide to Online Meeting Platforms, 10 Ways to Use a Spectrogram Online): bit.ly/lgo-tools

Facilitating online meetings & trainings (tips from Gastivists): bit.ly/lgo-facilitating

Coaching Online

Tips for coaching remote teams online: bit.ly/lgo-remote

Event Organizers

A Comprehensive List of Tips, Tools, and Examples for Event Organizers During the Coronavirus Outbreak: bit.ly/lgo-lgo-events

Mutual Aid Resources

Mutual Aid: How to Build a Network in Your Neighborhood: bit.ly/lgo-mutualaid

Online space to discuss mutual aid: bit.ly/lgo-discuss

Mental health

Isolation Toolkit, tips for staying at home, doing physical distancing correctly, and managing your mental health: bit.ly/lgo-isolation

Free resources to do inside your home to stay sane, by Nim Ralph: bit.ly/lgo-freeresources

Digital Security

Digital Security Basics for Campaigners: bit.ly/lgo-security

Digital Resilience in the Time of Coronavirus: bit.ly/lgo-security2

Equipment and Visual Recommendations

PowerLabs' mic and camera recommendations: bit.ly/lgo-mic

SlidesGo.com — free beautiful google slides and powerpoint presentations: bit.ly/lgo-slides

The contributors

Jeanne Rewa (co-author) is the Online Training Coordinator at Training for Change and leads trainer development with PeoplesHub.org.

In 2014 she shifted entirely to online facilitation and training work. She now supports people all around the world to bring love, collaboration, equity, embodiment, creativity, experiential education and conflict engagement into online spaces. She's been working on a book about it but didn't finish by the time the pandemic struck. *Sign-up to hear about it at LeadingGroupsOnline.org.*

Jeanne is also a part-time artist and active in social justice and climate justice organizing in her community in Indiana.

Once the pandemic is over, she's looking forward to again hosting with her partner monthly activist potlucks under the full moon.

Daniel Hunter (co-author) is Associate Director of Global Trainings with 350.org and Curriculum Designer Extraordinaire at Sunrise Movement.

He has spent his life supporting grassroots activists all over the globe to express their full hearts in organizing and social change. True to his personal style, he wrote a fun, true-life story of how campaigning looks like in *Strategy and Soul*. He's written handbooks for specific movements with *Building a Movement to End the New Jim Crow* and *Climate Resistance Handbook: Or, I was part of a climate action. Now what?*

When he started at 350 he was challenged to facilitate online more. That inspired him to build Trainings.350.org, which has online and offline facilitation tools. He even developed free online courses called "Online Skill-ups" which teach campaigning, social movements, and climate science.

Once the pandemic is over, he's looking forward to hugging friends, watching movies, and worrying less.

Daphne Philippoussis (artist) is a visual artist who loves exploring the arts — either in music or fine arts. She loves Margaret Atwood and rain hitting her window. In theory, she is studying at Tyler School of Art at Temple University.

You can see more of her artwork on instagram at @killedmykactus. Or you can email her at dphilippoussis@icloud.com.

Once the pandemic is over she's looking forward to drinking coffee with grandmothers and experiencing a college learning community with friends.